This book is based on the song "How Do You Stand Out?" Copyright © 2023 Scott Jablonski. All rights reserved. Words and music written and performed by Scott Jablonski. Recorded by Justin Capaldi at Let's Rock Studio. Mixed by Tony Ricci at TRIAD Recording. Available on streaming platforms everywhere.

I'd like to Acknowledge Zdenek Sasek for his playful, relevant, and entertaining images as well as Nuria Corba for her step by step guidance in creating and publishing a children's book.

Thank you

Visit **www.scottjablonski.com** for more information.

First Scott Jablonski Publication Edition

ISBN- 13: 979-8862989038

Written by Scott Jablonski
Published by Scott Jablonski, RI USA

This book is dedicated to Maria, mia Bina. You stand out in so many ways as a wife, mom, daughter, sister, friend, doctor and overall human being.

Hey! I've got some news for you.

The words I
speak
I know are
true.

Ever since you were a little child
talent's been in you all the while

have you made

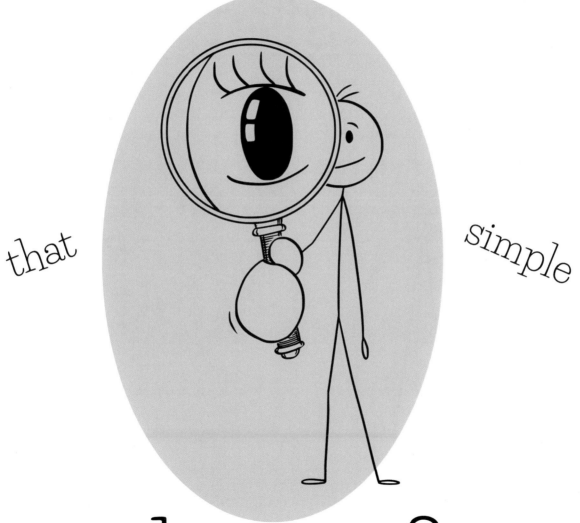

that

simple

discovery?

How do you **stand out?**

Go let the whole world see.

Yes, YOU stand out

just

like

a

Redwood

tree.

How do you <u>stand out</u>?

Go let the whole world see.

Always

strive

for

excellence!

Exercise with diligence.

Eat right.
Sleep tight.
Finish what you start.

In others
try to see the good

Learn new things you always should

Treat <u>everyone</u> kindly

follow
your
heart!!

How do you **stand out**?

Go let the whole world see.

We're all standouts

him her you and me.

Yes, you <u>stand</u> <u>out</u>

just like a Redwood tree.

How do you **stand out**?

Go let the whole world see.

Hopefully you've learned something new

with this
insight
what are you
going to do?

What can you start

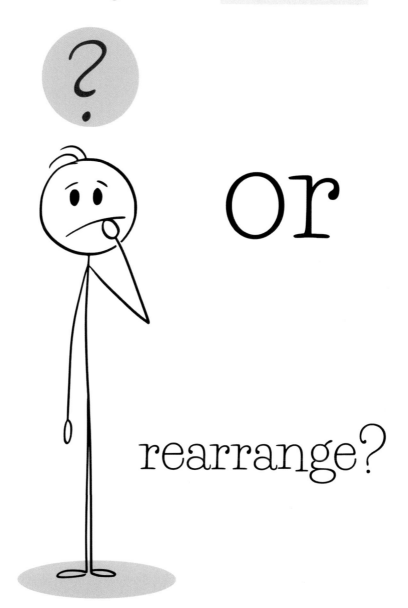

or

rearrange?

Why not begin as soon as you can?

Start now

today

Carpe diem!

Who can you help?

What can you change?

How do you **stand out?**

Go

let

the

whole

world

see.

We're all STANDOUTS

him

her

you and me.

Yes, you stand out

just

like

a

Redwood

tree.

How do you **stand out**?

Go let the whole world see!

you...

uniquely

How do **YOU**

<u>Glossary</u>

<u>carpe diem</u>- (seize the day) doing something now, not putting it off until later then regretting not doing it

<u>diligence</u>- consistent and focused hard work

<u>insight</u>- something powerful you have learned about yourself or something else

<u>stand out</u>- being different from everything and everyone else in a positive and productive way

<u>talent</u>- something you naturally do really well, you love doing and it and people take notice

<u>uniquely</u>- how you do something in a different, special, one-of-a-kind way

Stand Out! Stand Out!
The "8 Do Always" Framework

S trive for excellence
T ake great care of yourself
A lways do what you say you'll do
N otice and tell when others do well
D o what's right

O pen up your mind
U se your talents to do good things
T reat <u>everything</u> with respect and
be kind!

About the Author

Scott is a teacher, author and songwriter whose work is aimed at helping children become their best version. Seeing the potential in every child, he is passionate about creating content that builds character and promotes positive habits inspiring our youth to make a difference in the world.

His works are designed to be shared by parents, grandparents, caregivers, guardians, teachers and coaches all working with children toward the same positive goal.

Scott lives in Rhode Island with his wife, two sons and their Double Doodle dog Sammie. When not creating "Edutainment" for kids, Scott enjoys hiking and running on wooded trails, travel, landscaping, exercise, reading and devouring chocolate!

Made in the USA
Middletown, DE
28 October 2023

40941887R00020